BEN STOKES

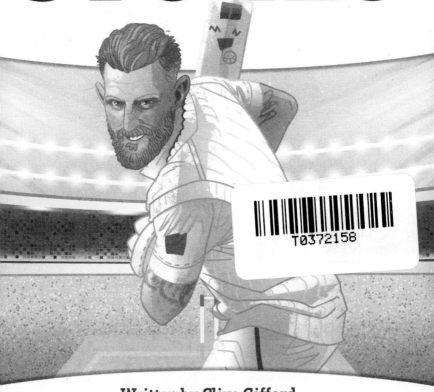

Written by Clive Gifford

RED■
SHED

CHAPTER 1

By the Barest of Margins

Four hard years of work, seven weeks of competition, 99.5 overs of tough cricket on the day and it all came down to this: 14 July, in front of a packed crowd at Lord's Cricket Ground in London, Ben Stokes faced the final ball of the 2019 ICC World Cup Final and the whole of England – as well as New Zealand – held its breath.

The previous ball had seen Adil Rashid lose his wicket: run out as he and Ben had strived to add two to the score. Ben's heart was still thumping from sprinting those runs . . . and from the hugeness of the occasion. England were

241–9, needing two runs to win, one to tie and with only one wicket left. Any mistake could cost the match and the last man in was Mark Wood – 'Woody' – the lovable, lightning-fast bowler who was also Ben's pal and teammate at Durham.

Each team in a Cricket World Cup One Day International (ODI) match gets 50 overs to compile as big a score as possible or chase down their opponent's total to win. The World Cup was first held in 1975 and England had never been champions, although they had come desperately close, losing in the final three times.

"Come on England!"

Ben had been in good form throughout the tournament. He'd struck 89 versus South Africa in England's opening game, and added scores of 79 (v India), 82 (v Sri Lanka) and 89 again (v Australia). He didn't bat in the semi-final as England trounced their oldest cricketing rival, Australia, by reaching their target of 223 with more than 17 overs to spare – an absolute thrashing. How England loved knocking their old foe out with ease!

But the final was proving to be a much tighter, nerve-jangling contest.

In front of almost 30,000 fans, England had bowled well to keep New Zealand's score down to 241, but they'd struggled in their run chase on a sticky pitch. They were 86–4 until hard-hitting Jos Buttler and Ben put on a stellar partnership of 110 runs. But then Jos fell, skying a ball high into the air for New Zealand quick bowler Tim Southee to catch. Chris Woakes, Liam Plunkett and Jofra Archer all followed. It had been left to Ben to score the remaining runs as evening loomed and the crowd worked itself into a frenzy.

Fifteen runs were still needed off the last over, to be bowled by the Kiwis' premier fast bowler, Trent Boult. Ben spoke to his batting partner, Adil Rashid. "I need to take all six balls – so no running, unless we can get two." Adil nodded and settled nervously at the non-striker's end. Could Stokesy do it?

49.1: Ben strikes the ball but sees it is heading to a New Zealand fielder. He decides not to run so he can keep the strike and face the next ball.

49.2: Trent bowls a good delivery which Ben gets his bat on but fails to score from. Now, it's 15 runs off just four balls . . . and the pressure is mounting.

49.3: Down goes Ben on one knee: a slog-sweep, and up, up and away flies the ball. It sails high over the midwicket boundary. The crowd roars. SIX!

49.4: Ben pushes the ball, the pair run two but as the throw is returned, it hits

Ben's outstretched bat and cannons off to the boundary. Ben apologises – he knew nothing about it as the ball had been thrown from behind him – but four is still added to the two that he and Adil ran. ANOTHER SIX!

49.5: Again, Ben and Adil go for two, but this time Adil is run out. Nooo!

49.6: The final ball. Ben drives it low on the leg side, mindful of not getting out Caught and losing England the game. He and Woody sprint for their lives . . . the pair manage one run to level the scores, but Jimmy Neesham had gathered the ball and hurled it towards Trent Boult who was lurking by the stumps. Woody, knowing he was short, desperately hurled himself forward into a full-length dive . . . but Trent had gathered the ball and clattered the stumps.

OUT! The game was tied.

Ben was furious and kicked his bat 10 metres away with frustration. Woody picked himself up and ran up to him. "Mate, you've been absolutely fantastic. You've given us a chance of winning." But Ben felt he'd let the team down.

One Day International Cricket was now entering uncharted territory. For the first time in 4,129 ODI matches, a game would be decided by a Super Over. Each team could pick any pair of batters to face six balls. Whoever scores the most runs, wins. England were to bat first.

Ben and Woody returned to an England dressing room in chaos. Players were scrabbling for their kit and hotly debating what should be done. Ben needed a moment to regain focus.

Adrenaline surged through him. He needed
to get a calm head, so he took himself off into
the showers for five minutes.

England's captain, Eoin Morgan, remained
ice-cool though. He wanted a left-hander
and a right-hander to bat and chose Jos Buttler
and Ben. Even though he suggested Jason Roy
instead of himself, Ben marched out with Jos.
He would do whatever the captain demanded
and the team wanted.

The pair scored 15 runs, which felt a formidable
total until Jimmy Neesham hit a six off Jofra
Archer in New Zealand's reply. Suddenly,
New Zealand needed just seven off four balls,
then five off three, then just two off the final ball.
Lord's fell silent.

The ground was half bathed in sunlight, half
in shadow, as Jofra Archer hurtled in to bowl.

Martin Guptill hit the ball out towards deep
midwicket as Jason Roy sped in from the
boundary to field.

J-Roy hurled the ball towards Jos Buttler, England's wicketkeeper, as the New Zealand batters ran hard . . .

As Jos gathered and smashed the stumps with the ball, TV commentator Ian Smith roared, *"ENGLAND HAVE WON THE WORLD CUP! BY THE BAREST OF MARGINS! BY THE BAREST OF ALL MARGINS!"*

There was nothing between the two teams. Both had scored 241 off 50 overs and then 15 off their Super Over, but the winner was decided by the team who had scored the most boundaries – New Zealand had struck 17, England, 26, seven of which were Ben's.

Ben sprinted across the ground to join a gaggle of his teammates. Everyone was going wild.

England had won the Cricket World Cup for the first time in front of a spellbound audience. The game was considered the most exciting in Cricket World Cup history and New Zealand-born Ben was awarded Man of the Match.

Hours later, England's dressing room was rowdy and packed with players, their families and the trophy. They only left when Lord's closed down at midnight, filling the air with songs and cheers.

"Brilliant, Stokesy!"

"Well played, Jofra!"

"We are the Champions!"

"*Allez! Allez! Allez!*"

"It's coming! Cricket's coming home!"

The England players marvelled at the game and Ben in their post-match interviews.

"I thought I'd seen everything in cricket, but that game was just ridiculous," chuckled Jos Buttler.

Joe Root, Ben's great mate on the team, singled him out. "It's almost written in the stars for Ben. Everything he's gone through – I can't be more proud and pleased for him."

The captain, Eoin Morgan, called him, "almost superhuman".

Ben, though, wasn't going to let all the praise get to his head and recalled the words he had spoken quietly to Jofra just before the young pace bowler bowled the Super Over.

"Everyone believes in you. Whatever happens here – this isn't going to define your career."

Ben knew only too well how cricket produced crushing lows as well as incredible highs, and how what you learned from the lows can help improve you as a cricketer. In Ben's case, he only had to think back three years to a previous World Cup Final . . .

CHAPTER 2

World Cup Low

"Typical Rooty, scampering quick singles," thought Ben on the balcony as his mate, Joe Root, top scored for England with 54. Ben had only contributed 13 runs before a good length ball from West Indian quick Dwayne Bravo had smashed into his stumps.

The game was the ICC World Twenty20 Final in 2016. England had cruised to the final with Joe Root shining throughout. Now, in front of 66,000 fans at Eden Gardens in Kolkata, Ben and the rest of the team had the chance to go for glory and win a major competition.

England only managed a modest total of

155 in warm, sticky conditions. The Eden Gardens pitch was pretty flat and good for batting, so it would need something special from Ben and the rest of the bowlers and fielders to stop the West Indies from passing England's total.

It came in the second over from their surprising skipper, Eoin Morgan. He brought on Joe to bowl. "Why not Moeen Ali?" Ben had thought as he trotted to field at mid-on. Seconds later, the ball flew gently straight into Ben's hands. Joe had taken a wicket with his first ball! "Morgs, you genius," Ben cheered as the team huddled together.

Next in to bat was Chris Gayle – the 'Universe Boss' – and one of the deadliest T20 hitters in the game. To prove the point, Gayle pummelled the first ball he faced for a powerful four.

Joe's next ball was also smashed high, but this time towards the long on boundary . . . where Ben was now fielding. He moved sharply and took a great catch. Two down in two overs. And then David Willey reduced the Windies to 11–3 in the next over. Brilliant!

Marlon Samuels rebuilt the innings with a great knock of 85, but with just one over to go the West Indies needed 19 runs, and their batters would be facing Ben.

Eoin gave Ben a look. Both felt confident as Ben had bowled the last over in the previous two matches for England and they'd gone really well.

In the first game, Sri Lanka had needed 15 runs to win with their dangerous all-rounder, Angelo Mathews, at the crease. Ben managed to bowl six near-perfect deliveries right at Angelo's feet, making it impossible to hit a big boundary shot. Ben's over cost just four runs. England were through to the semis!

Then, in the semi-final, Ben bowled two all-action overs at the end, taking three wickets and running out a further New Zealander

(Mitchell McClenaghan) with a direct hit on the very last ball. Game over and England were into the final.

So, Ben was confident – even though facing him was young all-rounder Carlos Brathwaite. Carlos was in his first international competition and his powerful frame made Ben think that he could hit – and hit big. He'd have to bowl pitch-perfect yorkers to keep Carlos quiet. Carlos, for his part, sought advice from his more experienced batting partner. Marlon Samuels' reply was just four words: "Swing for the hills!"

Ben ran in and bowled the first ball. It was a poor delivery, a little short and looping to the leg side. With a meaty swing, Carlos hoisted the ball up and over the leg side boundary for six runs. The crowd erupted.

Thirteen needed.

Ben walked back to the start of his bowling run up. "Okay, a bad ball. It happens." But Carlos struck his next delivery to the boundary as well.

World Cup Low

An enormous 94 metre-long hit resulted in six more!

"We can still win this," Ben thought, hands on his hips. "I just need to get the next one right."

He bounded in again and released a straighter, fuller ball. It was a better delivery and Carlos swung hard. "He's miss-hit the ball," Ben thought excitedly, spotting the bat handle turn in Carlos' hands. But such was Carlos' power, it still sailed over the boundary, landing 15 rows back. Wow!

Ben rubbed the sweat from his face and hair. He could barely think. Meanwhile in the TV commentary box, David Lloyd sighed, "Taken away in the final over. England are shell-shocked."

The scores were now level and Ben had a dreadful feeling in the pit of his stomach as he bowled his fourth ball. Away it went again. SIX MORE! The West Indies had won.

The England players bowed their heads or sprawled on the turf. Ben wanted the ground to open up and swallow him. He had let his team down. Even a consoling hug from Joe didn't help.

Minutes later, he sat in the changing room with a towel over his head.

"Unlucky, Ben."

"Chin up."

J-Roy, Moeen and the rest of the team patted him on the shoulder or whispered words of support. "Losing this game isn't who you are," Ben thought. "Don't let this defeat swallow you up."

Knowing he'd soon have to go out and face the media and the wider world, he vowed to do two things. First, he wanted people to know he was hurt, but positive and not sulking. Second, he wanted to congratulate Carlos on his match-winning innings of 34 off just 10 balls and hand him his Stokes 55 shirt. "It's what you do in cricket – you respect your opponent and their performances."

Later that night, sitting with his team singing

karaoke, Ben reached for his smartphone. There were dozens of kind texts and positive messages of support from cricketers, friends, fans, plus one from Australian bowling legend Shane Warne.

"It is hurting at the moment. Head high. Use tonight's match as motivation on every level so you don't feel like this again."

It proved to be brilliant advice.

★ CHAPTER 3 ★

Wanna Play Cricket?

"Wanna play cricket?"

Visitors to Deb and Ged Stokes' home in Christchurch, New Zealand, in the early 1990s would be pestered with this question by a young boy, swinging a yellow plastic toy cricket bat. Visitors were instructed to bowl the ball down the narrow hallway of the bungalow. Benjamin Andrew Stokes would swing his toy bat and slam the ball back down the hall with a ferocious straight drive.

"How could such a young kid strike the ball so hard and straight?" many wondered. Even more extraordinary was that Ben began his hallway cricket career whilst he was still in nappies and not yet three years old. (Then again, when your dad was a professional rugby league player and your mother was an international youth basketball player and cricketer, perhaps it's far less of a surprise.) Pre-school Ben couldn't sit still and loathed being left in his room.

"Let me out! Let me go!"

"Ben, stop shouting."

"But Mam, I want to go out and play."

Even before he'd reached school age, Ben frequently went missing. Time and time again, his worried parents or neighbours had to go out looking for him.

Once, Ben's mum Deborah was fretting over Ben's latest disappearance when she discovered him sitting on top of their carport roof. He was only three – how did he get up there?

As Ben grew up, his hallway cricket and roof climbing were replaced with family contests in the back garden. James was seven years older than Ben, so it was hardly a fair match-up, but Ben started to compete well against his half-brother – with the odd broken window resulting.

Ben's dad, Gerard 'Ged' Stokes, was an incredibly tough rugby league forward. He appeared four times for New Zealand and regularly for Canterbury and Eastern Suburbs. Whilst playing for Canterbury against Wellington in 1982, Ged suffered an agonising injury: he dislocated the middle finger of his left hand.

"I thought to myself, 'I don't really want to come off for a dislocated finger,' so I put it back in myself," Ged told rugby league writer John Coffey later.

Unfortunately, he didn't do a good job and the finger popped out of its joint a second time. So, Ged slammed it back in again . . . and again. Ow! By the end of the game, his finger was badly broken and sticking out at an angle.

Ged continued playing matches but found

his damaged finger got in the way, so he ordered a surgeon to cut it off! Ged told his family a different story, though. He claimed it was bitten off by a crocodile! Ben believed his dad's tall tale for many years.

Losing a finger was just one of many injuries Ged suffered, including a broken jaw and nose, and fractures of his skull. The most serious occurred 11 days after Ben was born (4 June 1991), when Ged broke his neck during a match. His playing career was over, so, to support his young family, he turned to coaching rugby and working as a carpenter and plasterer.

Ben loved going to jobs with his dad. When Ged renovated the family's bungalow in Christchurch, eight-year-old Ben helped out by crawling under the floorboards to lay pipes and cables. When he went with his dad to rugby coaching sessions, he would practise kicking goals or sit and watch the team talks.

Rugby in New Zealand is even more popular

than football is in the UK. It's a way of life and is played everywhere and by everyone. Ben started playing – a sport where all his energy could be put to good use. He wouldn't stop tackling, and in one rugby league match for his local club, Marist, he scored six tries.

When Ben was 10, the family moved cities from Christchurch in New Zealand's South Island to Wellington in the North Island. Ged was now the assistant coach of the New Zealand national rugby league team and Ben hung out in the national team changing room all the time. The players didn't seem to mind, and they treated him well.

Once, the team captain Ruben Wiki offered Ben his socks as a souvenir. Ben turned them down and said, "Nah, mate, I want your boots!" Cheeky.

Ben started playing rugby union at his school, Plimmerton, and rugby league for a local club, Porirua Vikings. Many of the young players were

Maori or Pacific islanders, so a new, fair-skinned redhead stood out.

"Who's that skinny white kid?"

"What, the one with red hair? Stokes. His dad played league."

"Look, he's gonna tackle the prop forward."

"He's crazy! He's gonna get mashed."

"Oooh. He got crunched."

"Stokes is broke! Ha, ha!"

"No, look, he's up and trying again. That kid is crazy tough."

Ben won them over with his all-energy displays. He would never give up and often sought out the bigger players on the other team to try to tackle. It didn't always work out and he had plenty of bumps, cuts and bruises to show for his efforts.

If playing rugby as often as possible was not enough, Ben was also keeping his cricket going. Plimmerton's cricket coach, Mike Smellie, was impressed by the new boy the first time he turned up at team trials.

"Young kids usually want to pull, hook and hit the ball behind square," he mused. "But this Ben Stokes is hitting the ball straight and out of the school ground, aged 10. He is absolutely smashing it."

Ben was a no-brainer pick for the school team and started powering the side to victory. Plimmerton was a smaller school than some of their opponents but that didn't stop them winning plenty of games in the national Milo Cup competition. When they did finally lose to the eventual champions, Palmerston North, Ben still scored a century – even though the day before his arm had still been in plaster after he'd broken it.

The cast was supposed to stay on for a further three weeks, but Ged saw to that. He grabbed some scissors and cut the cast off the night before the game, so eager was Ben to take part.

Things were happening for Ben. He was

getting noticed for his sporting prowess in both cricket and rugby. At the end of 2003, he was picked to play for the Wellington junior provincial cricket team – quite some achievement for a boy of 12. A certificate was prepared, but Ben wouldn't receive it for 19 years . . .

⭐ CHAPTER 4 ⭐

Voyage to the Other Side of the World

When Ben was 12, his world was turned upside-down.

In the 1980s, his father had played a season in England for Workington Town. Now, the club asked Ged to return to become head coach. Deb, Ged and Ben were to move to the other side of the world. Ged went first and Deb and Ben followed, leaving four days before Christmas Day 2003.

"No, Mam, no! NOOOOOOOOOO!"

Ben was devastated. He'd only just got truly settled in Wellington after the family's move from Christchurch.

Amazing Cricket Stars – Ben Stokes

The Stokes lived less than 200 metres from beautiful beaches in Porirua and not much farther away from the rugby and cricket grounds that Ben enjoyed so much. Ben knew nothing about Cumbria, a county tucked away in north-eastern England. But he did know he didn't want to move to the other side of the world, away from his friends and relatives. But it wasn't his choice.

Ben found himself living in Cockermouth, a market town close to the Lake District and surrounded by rugged countryside. It was neither a big place, nor were there many other towns close by. Ben grew to like the fact he got to know everyone there and, eventually, they all knew him.

At school, both kids and even one or two teachers mocked his New Zealand accent. Some of the kids found it funny when he pronounced his own name 'Bin' rather than 'Ben'.

"D'you spell your name B-I-N?"

"Hah! Rubbish Bin Stokes."

"Hey, Bin – are you rubbish?"

But the mocking didn't last long. It helped that there were plenty of kids who enjoyed playing sport, just like him. It didn't take long for him to start hanging out with half of the school cricket team: Hugh, Matty, Humayoon, Stuart and Greg. Stuart's dad Murray remembers Ben as "a nice lad, although he ate us out of house and home in biscuits!"

Ben's new schoolmates invited him down to winter nets at the local cricket club. His pals played for both the school and the club. He felt instantly at home, and soon he was crashing the ball down the rubber matting strip much like he used to straight down the hall in New Zealand when he was a toddler. Only now his technique and power were even more obvious to those looking on.

"Wow! Ben hits hard."

"That one really pinged off the bat."

"Good timing as well. Monster!"

Ben was fortunate to be in a great school year for cricket; his new mates were a talented bunch. Even though the school pitch was a tatty old piece of artificial turf, and they played in black trousers and polo shirts, not proper cricket gear, the team started to do well.

In his first full season, Cockermouth School became Cumbrian champions in a national schools competition run by the Lord's Taverners, a leading UK youth and disability sports charity. They did so by defeating Sedbergh, a wealthy private school with a long history of sporting success. Ben was a star that day, clearing the boundary time after time with big shots during his innings.

Ben was also invited to a two-day visit to Sedbergh. A sports scholarship might be offered if he proved good enough, but Ben had no intention of accepting: he was happy at Cockermouth and knew that posh blazers, shirts

and ties were not for him. He did leap at
the chance of the visit, though, as it meant
two days off school and another chance to
play cricket!

Ben was already clear in his mind that he
wanted to be a sportsperson when he grew
up. He simply didn't enjoy school lessons and
found it hard to concentrate on schoolwork
for long periods of time. He wasn't naughty –
well, not that naughty – he did get sent to the
headmaster's study a few times.

"What are you here for, Stokes?"

"Didn't do my homework, sir."

"Why not?"

"Dunno, sir."

"Come on now, Ben. Don't like it here?
I heard you've made friends."

"Yeah, they're great. No, it's good here.
I just . . ."

"Speak up, boy."

"I prefer playing sport, sir."

Ben did get a few detentions, but he wasn't a bully, or disruptive in class. He simply didn't do the work he should. His heart and mind were set solely on playing sport, hoping it would become his career.

As soon as the bell rang for PE, Ben was up and out of his seat. He was often first in the changing room, kitted out and ready to train or play. His PE teacher, Mr Hayes, found him a willing student, always ready to learn by doing, and keen to be in the thick of the action.

⭐ CHAPTER 5 ⭐

The Mystery Donor

Whilst Ben played lots of sports at school and at Broughton Red Rose rugby league club, his favourite place quickly became the cricket club at Cockermouth. It was where he felt at home. Most days after school, he'd burst out of the school gates, trot down Castlefield Drive, cross the bridge over the River Derwent and head straight into the ground on Gote Road where he'd play in the nets for hours.

Whack!

"Is that the best ball you've got?"

Whack!

"Four! I thought you were a fast bowler!"

Swish . . .

"Fair play, lad. Good delivery."

On Saturdays, Ben couldn't wait to get to the ground. He'd stay there all day, hoping to get a game and a chance to shine. His dad bought him fizzy drinks at the club's bar, into which Ben would dunk a Mars bar . . . Urgh!

Whilst playing cricket for the juniors, there was a rule that a batter had to retire once they had scored 29 runs. This was to give other young players a chance to have a go. Ben didn't break the rule, but he would often manipulate his score to reach 28 runs, then try to launch a giant six to finish his innings.

His adventurous play and raw talent caught the eye of local cricket coach Jon Gibson, who watched him in sessions in the nets. Ben bowled right-handed and batted left-handed. Nothing wrong in that. Quite a lot of players do, including Stuart Broad, Travis Head and Moeen Ali.

The coach thought Ben was exciting but still had much to learn. He bowled fast but his aim was erratic – the ball might fly either side of the stumps. His batting could also be hit or miss. He loved thumping the ball as hard as possible but his defence and shot selection needed plenty of work. Coach Gibson started teaching Ben more delicate shots and how to place the ball. Ben was fascinated by the coach's tips, and he practised hard.

Things were not going so well for Ben's father, however. Ged was sacked as coach of Workington Town and the family struggled to make ends meet. Ged and Deb even discussed returning to New Zealand but didn't want to uproot Ben again, especially as he was happy and developing his sporting prowess in Cumbria.

Help came in the form of a mysterious fan at Cockermouth. They donated money to pay for Ben to have one-to-one coaching sessions with Jon Gibson. All the mystery donor asked in return was to remain anonymous. Ben didn't know their identity for many years, and only he, Deb and Coach Gibson know who it is today – it's a very well-kept secret.

All the good coaching, hard work and practice started paying off. In 2006, Ben started getting picked for Cockermouth's first XI. He was so excited. The side contained plenty of experienced players, including captain Steve Chambers, who was 45 – three times Ben's age! But he wasn't the only teen on the team: there was his school classmate Greg Platten, as well as tearaway fast bowler Chris Hodgson, who was a year older.

The mix of young and old clicked and Cockermouth started beating everyone they played. They were competing in the tough North Lancashire and Cumbria Cricket League and stumbled in a big game against favourites Workington. They were battling for a draw when Ben came in to bat at number seven.

"I must get us over the line," he muttered to himself as another wicket fell.

The Mystery Donor

Ben did a brilliant job and was on 44 when he faced the last ball of the match. Cockermouth were nine wickets down so he couldn't afford to make a mistake. Then again, he had never made a 50 for the first team before and he sensed his chance . . .

As the bowler released the ball, Ben strode down the pitch, swung his bat and – CRUNCH! – drove the ball hard and straight.

Workington had two fielders on the boundary, but they needn't have bothered moving. The ball sailed high over their heads and thudded into a wall well beyond the rope. SIX! Ben had his 50 and Cockermouth their draw.

Looking on, Steve Chambers cursed then chuckled. "Wow! What sort of 15 year old does that?" He wouldn't be the last person to be surprised and awestruck by Ben's personality and cricketing prowess.

⭐ CHAPTER 6 ⭐

Rising Up

Ben continued appearing for his local cricket club, but other teams wanted him to play for them as well. Still in his mid-teens, Ben Stokes – the Kiwi from Christchurch, now Cockermouth – was in demand!

Ben was selected for the Cumbria youth team even though he was a year or two younger than many of the team. When Cumbria played Yorkshire, Ben encountered Joe Root for the first time. The pair met again at the Bunbury Festival for the best Under-15 cricketers in England, where Ben also encountered players like Jos Buttler, Sam Billings and Jack Leach.

Back in New Zealand, Ben had quickly ruined his first proper cricket bat by using it to hit stones instead of cricket balls. Even when he was playing for Cumbria, the team shared a couple of batting helmets rather than have their own. So, you can understand his amazement when cricket company Gray-Nicolls decided to sponsor him.

There'd be a day before the start of each season that felt like three Christmas Days all rolled into one. It was when the Gray-Nicolls catalogue dropped through the letterbox. Ben could select bats, clothing and protective gear for free. A-maz-ing!

Whilst playing for Cumbria against Durham Under-15s, Ben took three wickets for 28 runs. It wasn't long before John Windows, the head coach of Durham's academy, invited Ben to join. Unlike Cumbria, Durham was one of the 18 professional clubs in the County Championship. Although still at school, Ben leapt at the chance.

It felt as if his dream of playing cricket as a full-time job was one crucial step nearer.

The switch from Cumbria to Durham did, however, mean some very early starts for his poor parents as they ferried Ben cross-country from one side of England to the other. Some 180 kilometres lay between Cockermouth and Chester-le-Street, home to Durham County Cricket Club. There wasn't one big, fast motorway direct between the two places and the routes could be confusing if you hadn't lived there all of your life. Ged and Deb would often bicker in the car as another one of Deb's attempted shortcuts ended in confusion.

"Turn left."

"Where?"

"By that fence, up on the left."

"Right."

"No, I said left, Ged."

"I meant 'correct'. Heck, Deb, we're lost!"

Ben avoided the arguments, asleep in the

back seat of the family car. By now, he had chosen to give up rugby . . . and schoolwork. Ben left school at 16 with just one GCSE – in PE (not surprisingly). It did not reflect how intelligent he was, rather how little work he put in.

He didn't turn his back on Cockermouth, however. Firstly, he set up an award for the most resilient and hardworking under-13-year-old player at the club. He named the award the Kia Kaha Trophy, which means 'stay strong' in the Māori language. Then, when the club suffered disastrous floods a couple of years later, damaging the ground, Ben raced over from Durham to help in the clear-up campaign.

By 2009, Ben's career was blossoming at Durham. He passed through the academy and was playing regularly for the Second XI adult team. He had been very nervous before his Second XI debut in 2007 against Lancashire, but struck a brilliant hundred on the day. Out in the middle, he found he could treat any match as just another cricket game even when the stakes were raised. He also took plenty of wickets that year, including a great spell of 4–19 versus Leicestershire.

In May of 2009, he travelled down with Durham's first team to the famous Oval ground in south London. Durham were playing Surrey in a Friends Provident Trophy one day match and Ben got to bat (scoring 11 not out) and bowl. The third ball of his very first over crashed through Mark Ramprakash's defence and hit the stumps. The former England opening batter had played 52 Test matches for his country but had no answer to Ben's delivery.

The scorer noted down:

M.R. Ramprakash – bowled B.A. Stokes 36.

It was Ben's first senior adult wicket.

Later that year, after performing well in Second XI games, he got the offer all young cricketers yearn for. Durham awarded him a two-year professional contract. Durham had won the County Championship in both 2008 and 2009. Their squad was packed full of talent from Paul Collingwood and Steve Harmison, to young Australian batter David Warner and West Indian legend Shivnarine Chanderpaul. Ben knew he had a challenge on to break into the first team but couldn't wait for the new season to start.

★ CHAPTER 7 ★

Trials and Triumphs

Ben made his full debut for the Durham first team not in England or Wales but the Middle East. In March 2010, he scored 51 in his first innings against the MCC in a match held in Abu Dhabi. Two months later he scored his first century for Durham in the County Championship, against Nottinghamshire, bouncing back after the opposition batters had thumped his bowling to score 106 runs. Ben was buzzing.

Nottinghamshire's director of cricket Mick Newell was impressed with the young redhead that day, telling reporters, "Ben is going to be a fantastic cricketer. He is very self-motivated, very competitive . . . He's the all-round package and I'm sure he will be an international cricketer if he progresses the right way."

That winter, Mick Newell was in charge of the England Lions tour of the Caribbean. The Lions are an England 'B' team designed to give mostly up-and-coming cricketers a taste of international cricket.

Ben was thrilled to be selected as part of the Lions squad alongside Jonny Bairstow, Steven Finn and Ravi Bopara, amongst others. At 19, he was the baby of the squad and only played in three of the games, but it was exciting to represent England and mix with other talented players.

Training for the tour, though, was a bit of a rude awakening. Ben saw just how much fitter and more focused some of his teammates were and realised he had some catching up to do. And there was more! England's coaches commented that Ben could lose some weight.

Ben knew they were right as he didn't pay as much attention to what he ate as he should. So he set about getting fitter, eating better, and lost 15 kilograms over the next year.

"In the gym again, Ben?"

"You betcha!"

"Beer and pie for tea?"

"Nope. Chicken and pasta. Yum!"

When he returned to Durham for the 2011 season, there were comments about his weight loss in the first team dressing room.

"Blimey, didn't they feed you on the Lions tour?"

"Got rid of the baby fat at last!"

"Ben-ch-Press Stokes, more like. Look at that muscle."

"Guess you'll only be bowling pies, now, not eating them!"

Ben laughed off the jokes. It was all good dressing room fun that made him feel part of the team. Inside, he truly felt fitter and sharper than ever and really excited for the season ahead.

In the very first County Championship game of 2011, Ben scored 135 not out against Hampshire – but that was only part of the story. After Ben scored his century just after tea, Hampshire brought on spin bowler Liam Dawson to try to stem the flow of runs. Ben was playing aggressively, without fear, and seeing the ball really well. He decided to go for it.

Dawson's first ball sailed through the air for a six. And the second, third and fourth!

Ben charged down the pitch or leant back and slog-swept, all shots clearing the boundary. Some of the crowd at the Rose Bowl began murmuring. They knew that only two players had ever hit six sixes in an over in first class cricket – Sir Garfield Sobers in 1968 and Indian all-rounder Ravi Shastri in 1985.

"That Durham kid's going to match Sobers and Shastri."

"Oh, the nerve of him. He's still a teenager."

Trials and Triumphs

"Awesome power for a youngster."

Ben also felt the record was on, especially when he sent the fifth ball into the stands. The pitch was good and the weather warm and clear – excellent for batting.

"Liam, Liam!" The Hampshire captain Nic Pothas called his bowler over for a chat. The game ground to a halt. The wily opposition skipper slowed everything down, leaving Ben to pace up and down like a caged animal ready to strike again.

The conference between captain and bowler worked. Dawson bowled his final delivery. It was a quick ball aimed at Ben's feet – very hard to score from – and he could only work the ball away for a single.

"Still, 31 runs off a single over," he thought. "Can't be bad." But he was disappointed he didn't match the record.

Earlier that day, Ben had starred with the ball just when Durham really needed him to.

Their main fast bowler, Steve Harmison, suffered an arm injury and Ben was thrown the ball by skipper Phil Mustard. Ben responded with three wickets early on and then came on to bowl at Derbyshire's England legend Dominic Cork . . .

"Howzat, Umps?" Ben roared an appeal for leg before wicket. The umpire raised his finger. Cork was out.

The next batter in was Danny Briggs. Ben dismissed him for a duck after a smart catch by Durham's captain (and wicketkeeper) Phil Mustard.

Last man in for Hampshire was Simon Jones, the former England pace bowler. He survived the first ball but not the second, as Ben's delivery smashed his stumps. Out!

"Brilliant, Ben!" shouted his teammates. That was three wickets in just five balls, with innings figures of six for 68. He'd taken more wickets in one innings then he had taken for the Durham first class team during the whole previous season! Throw in his century as well and it was no surprise he woke up to appreciative headlines in the next day's newspapers.

Stokes' Day

Ben Stokes Shows His England Potential

Stokes Puts Hampshire to the Sword

Whilst Ged and Deb Stokes were thrilled with the praise in the papers, Ben was more bothered that his performances hadn't gained Durham the win (Hampshire had clung on for a draw). Ben always put the team result ahead of his own personal performance. However, he continued his good form in the early months of the season, hitting a watchful 120 against Somerset and blasting a career high 185 against Lancashire.

Drama occurred though when it was Durham's turn to field against Lancashire. As he swooped to attempt a low catch, Ben felt an agonising crack in his right index finger. The ball had hit the end of his finger and dislocated it. He left the field to see the team physio – he wasn't going to pop it back in himself like his dad did all those years ago. But just like Ged's injury, the finger stubbornly refused to stay in place. So, off to the hospital he had to go. There, X-rays confirmed that the joint was shattered and Ben would need an operation.

Another followed, which left him out of action for the next eight weeks . . . just as he was playing well and building his place in the Durham team. So frustrating.

Not long after his comeback, he received a great surprise. He was picked for the England One Day International team in an August mini-tournament featuring Ireland and India. The month after, he got to play his first T20 international match, versus the West Indies, for England as well.

That index finger continued to prove

troublesome, though, especially after it got hit by a ball in the nets. Ben had to pull out of one of the T20 matches and the England doctors were clear – he needed a *third* operation on the finger. What a pain! This one involved Ben flying to the United States where specialists who worked with National Basketball Association stars performed complex surgery.

⭐ CHAPTER 8 ⭐

Three Lions

Ben got his first tattoo before he was 18 years old. He had to ask his mum's permission.

"Do think about it carefully," she urged.

"Choose a design that really means something to you."

He already considered himself English and was desperate to play for his adopted country. But he was also proud of where he had come from and his Māori heritage on his mother's side. In the end he opted for a number of Māori symbols pieced together to look like rugby balls, along with three lions – a symbol of England.

Ben would later add many tattoos, including the numbers 58 and 221, his player numbers for the England T20 and ODI teams. These would be followed in 2013 by the number 658. All England cricketers are listed by when they were first selected to play Tests for their country – Geoff Cook, Ben's coach at Durham, was number 493 and James Anderson was 613, for example. Ben was selected in late 2013 and became England's 658th Test cricketer. The 657th player had been Chris Woakes, and Ben's friend, Joe Root, was 655th.

By now, Ben had become a father. He'd met trainee teacher Clare Ratcliffe whilst playing a 2010 cricket match at Old Trafford and the pair had their first child in 2012, a boy they named Layton. Ben cried when his son was born, and also when daughter Libby followed in 2014. In between, Ben had been part of a Durham side that won the 2013 County Championship, winning 10 and drawing two of their 16 matches.

Three Lions

New dad Ben's first England Test match would be against the old enemy – Australia in the Ashes. The oldest and most famous Test series, the Ashes began in 1877 and is now a five-match series played every two years or so.

Ben wasn't selected for the first Ashes Test (which England lost) but during training for the second Test at the Adelaide Oval, England skipper Alastair Cook pulled him aside.

"You'll be making your debut, batting at six," said Captain Cook. Ben was delighted.

The Adelaide Oval is one of the most beautiful cricket grounds in Australia. Located in parklands, it still features an original scoreboard from 1911. On the first days of the Test, the scorers inside had their work cut out as Australia kept the runs flowing.

Ben felt he wasn't bowling well. His deliveries weren't threatening the Australian batters as much as he'd have liked. Michael Clarke reached his century, clipping a ball from Ben away, and Brad Haddin was on 51 as Ben began his 11th over.

With Australia 367 for 5, Ben finally found his rhythm. He released a good ball, Haddin edged it and wicketkeeper Matt Prior caught it in his gloves.

Ben was embraced by Alastair Cook, then Joe Root and Jimmy Anderson.

HE HAD TAKEN HIS FIRST TEST WICKET!

Or had he?

As Brad Haddin walked off the pitch, umpire Marais Erasmus checked the video replay and called the Australian batter back. Ben had overstepped the crease – it was a no ball. Drat! Ben was furious with himself and his mood turned worse when Brad started taking the mickey.

"That's your first and last Test wicket, mate." Brad grinned at Ben.

The umpire had to keep the two players apart.

"Calm down, Stokesy."

"Focus lad. Get him next ball."

Still furious, Ben bowled the next few balls at high speed but failed to make a breakthrough. It would be a further 25 overs before he was asked by his captain to start another spell of bowling.

Ben bounded in, Michael Clarke spooned the ball up in the air and Jimmy Anderson dived forward. Ben saw the whole thing in slow motion.

"Please hold on, Jimmy, please."

Umpire Kumar Dharmasena raised his finger.

Out! Jimmy had caught it! Ben finally had his first Test wicket and it was Australia's captain. He snared Peter Siddle later that day to end with 2 for 70 from 18 hard bowled overs. He only scored 1 and 28 in his two innings as England went 2–0 down in the series. Test cricket was hard!

Australia's leading paceman Mitchell Johnson was bowling fast, hostile and sometimes unplayable deliveries, taking 19 wickets in just two Tests. Some thought that a handful of his spells were the fastest they'd ever seen. So, when the England team viewed the hard, bouncy pitch at WACA before the third Test, some players were dismayed.

"It's rock hard. I've seen softer concrete."

"Look at those cracks – they're bound to widen."

"What will Johnson do on this?"

What Johnson did was take Ben's wicket in the first innings for 18. By the time he got to bat again, England were in deep trouble and the pitch cracks had widened and deepened. When the ball hit one of these, it bounced almost sideways. Lethal! Ben vowed to attack Mitchell Johnson and the rest of Australia's bowlers. He wasn't going to buckle and give his wicket away limply.

Balls whistled past his head as Johnson pounded in, bowling fiercely at high speed. Ben hooked and pulled some of the fastest deliveries, scoring quick runs off the snarling fast bowler. The Barmy Army – made up of diehard England fans – cheered his progress on.

Three Lions

They even broke into a song for Ben based on the 'Hokey Cokey' tune.

You put the batter in,
He bowls them out.
In, out, in, out, he swings it all about!
You do the Stokey Cokey and you
turn around,
That's what it's all about!
Oooooooh, the Stokey Cokey!

Ben loved it.

He reached a half century, then 70, 80, and on into the 'nervous nineties'. Mitchell Johnson returned with a barrage of short-pitched bowling. Many batters would try to avoid the bouncers. Not Ben. He took them on, pulling two short balls for two runs each then, as Mitchell released another pacy delivery, thumping it for a powerful boundary.

He'd done it! A CENTURY FOR ENGLAND!

Ben punched the air, high-fived Tim Bresnan and held his bat up in front of Mitchell Johnson as the crowd applauded. He wanted to show the Aussies that he wasn't easily beaten.

Ben eventually made 120 but England went 3–0 down, which became 4–0, then 5–0. The whitewash hurt but at least he was one of the few players who came out of the tour with credit, especially after he took six wickets in an innings in the fifth Test.

★ CHAPTER 9 ★

Broken Dreams

Just a couple of months later, Ben should have still been on a high. He'd played his first Tests, scored his first Test century and earned plenty of praise on an otherwise dismal tour.

The trouble was he was suffering a major slump in form. He felt great when practising in the nets but kept on getting out cheaply. He was finding it VERY frustrating.

All cricketers have periods when they're not scoring as freely as they would like. Ben had not been in great form for Durham for parts of the 2013 season and had talked things out with his captain, Paul Collingwood. But this time, he just couldn't shake off the feeling of failure.

Things seemed to get worse and worse on England's 2014 tour to the West Indies. Ben failed to take wickets and only scored 19 runs in seven innings. He was feeling the pressure, especially with the ICC World Twenty20 in Bangladesh only a few weeks away. Ben desperately wanted to appear in a World Cup for the first time.

"I mustn't fail," Ben thought as he marched out to the middle of the famous Kensington Oval in Barbados. Jos Buttler had just been caught and England, on 129–4, were having a bit of a wobble.

Krishmar Santokie bowled a slower ball. Ben tried to get his bat on it, but it turned past the inside edge and struck his middle stump.

HOWZAT!

There was no need for an appeal; Ben was out first ball without scoring – a golden duck. He stomped off past the team dugout by the boundary, not catching the supportive shouts of the crowd or his teammates as he walked into the England dressing room.

"Unlucky, Ben. Santo's bowling well."

"It was a good ball, Stokesy. Next time."

"Chin up, lad."

"Oh dear – looks like Ben's lost it."

Ben stormed over to his locker. He couldn't stop himself, he thumped the locker door with the heel of his palm as hard as he could.

CRASH!

The locker glass shattered. "What an idiot I've been," he thought. He'd have to clear up the mess, but that would turn out to be the least of his worries.

Ben didn't get to see England's final over where Chris Jordan belted four sixes, but by the time England had to field, he knew he was in a lot of trouble. His wrist and hand throbbed in pain. He taped the wrist up but was asked to field at slip.

"I've broken my wrist," he whispered to Jos Buttler behind the stumps. Jos chuckled, thinking Ben was joking.

He really wasn't.

Having played rugby, Ben was used to dealing with pain, but this was agony. When he tried to field the ball, he knew it was too much. He walked off the pitch hurt and told the physio what he had done. X-rays confirmed he had broken his wrist and would be out for at least five to six weeks – missing his first World Cup.

Ben apologised to his teammates and told his parents; his father called him "a wally!" He gained the nickname Hurt Locker from the England players for a time. And in 2015, when England returned to the same ground in the West Indies, Ben walked into the dressing room to discover that England batter Ian Bell had taped a boxing glove to his locker.

CLICK!

Broken Dreams

Ben took a photo and made that image the screensaver on his phone.

"Ha, ha! Very funny, Bell-y."

★ CHAPTER 10 ★

Match-winner!

Ben's wrist healed, his form returned and by
the end of 2015 he was thought of as a world
class all-rounder. To opponents he was a serious
threat with the bat, ball and as a fielder. He
took an out-of-this world catch, for example,
during the 2015 Ashes Test at Trent Bridge.
The ball seemed to fly past Ben before his
dive and grab snared it, leaving Stuart Broad
open-mouthed in astonishment.

Even better was a leap, turn and one-handed
catch at the 2019 World Cup against South
Africa. Ben was on the boundary and turned a
likely six into a wicket in spectacular fashion. It

caused Nasser Hussain on TV to exclaim, "Oh! No, no way. You cannot do that, Ben Stokes. That is remarkable. That is one of the greatest catches of all time!"

Three years earlier, Ben was on a tour to South Africa, where he notched his highest First Class score – a monumental 258. His partner for much of that time, Jonny Bairstow, kept on muttering, "Shot, lad," every time Ben struck a boundary. And with Ben clubbing 11 sixes and an incredible 30 fours in his innings, he must have heard, "Shot, lad," a lot!

Records tumbled as Ben scored the most runs by any Test cricketer batting at number six. He and Jonny Bairstow (150 not out) together broke the record for the highest partnership for the sixth wicket (399). At one point, Ben managed to hit a six right out of the Cape Town ground and into the neighbouring brewery. Ben revealed later it was deliberate – he was aiming for it!

Match-winner!

Later in 2016, Ben starred in England's tour of Bangladesh, including an all-action performance in Chattogram where he took four wickets in Bangladesh's first innings, two crucial wickets in just three balls in the second innings and, in between, top-scored in the match with a blistering innings of 85 on a tricky pitch. In a lowish-scoring game (no innings reached 300), Ben's runs and his 4–26 eased England to victory. He capped off the year being named in both the World XI Test and World XI ODI teams. Ben was in the best XIs on the planet.

The following February was an amazing month for Ben and his family. He was appointed vice-captain of England whilst his great mate Joe Root succeeded Alastair Cook to become England's 80th Test captain. Ben was delighted for Joe and considered the vice-captaincy a great honour. If that wasn't enough, a week later, Ben became the highest paid English cricketer of all time.

The Indian Premier League is the richest T20 competition in world cricket. Before the start of each season, the IPL has an auction where the teams can buy players. Ben had never played in the IPL before but entered the auction. There was no guarantee of any of the eight teams actually buying him. Instead, a five-team bidding war broke out. It turned out everyone wanted a bit of Ben!

Ben had set his alarm back in England for 3.30 in the morning to follow the auction. "Complete carnage!" he gasped in astonishment as the bids flowed in. It looked like Sunrisers Hyderabad would secure Ben's services until a final, winning, bid came in from Rising Pune Supergiants of £1.7 million – even more than the fees paid for Indian superstars Virat Kohli and MS Dhoni.

Ben joined MS Dhoni along with Steve Smith and Faf du Plessis in the Supergiants squad. He shined in the field where he snaffled some great catches as well as grabbing 12 wickets.

Match-winner!

With the bat, he scored 316 runs, the highlight of which was his first century in any T20 competition.

It came against the Gujarat Lions, a side containing Brendon McCullum, Suresh Raina and Ravi Jadeja. Gujarat batted first with McCullum top scoring with 45 runs. The Lions set a total of 162 to win and soon had the Supergiants in terrible trouble at 10 for 3 when Ben strode out to the crease.

He was watchful at first but punched his fifth ball for four to really get going. He was joined by MS Dhoni in the fifth over. The Supergiants were four down and much relied on this pair.

Ben thumped two sixes off Ravi Jadeja.

"Great work, Ben."

"Thanks, MS. Still behind the run rate."

"Yes. Let's ramp it up."

Dhoni hit a great six off James Faulkner but mainly nudged ones and twos to leave the heavy hitting to his partner. Ben got into the seventies but in the 16th over, Dhoni lost his wicket and Ben started suffering with cramps in his legs. But he responded, thumping two huge sixes in the 18th over then a blistering four in the 19th over to reach his century in just 61 balls.

Ben's partner, Daniel Christian, hit the winning runs, making this match one of nine the Supergiants won that season. They finished IPL runners-up with Ben named the IPL's most valuable player – quite an achievement for someone making their competition debut.

He continued in great form throughout spring and summer 2017, scoring centuries in ODIs against South Africa and Australia, then two more hundreds in Tests, versus South Africa and West Indies. After scoring 73 in an England victory over the West Indies in September, he went out for the evening to celebrate with teammates. Later that night, he was arrested for an affray (fight) in Bristol.

Ben denied he was guilty of starting the brawl, but CCTV footage showed him throwing punches. He was dropped from the England team and told he would not be playing in that winter's Ashes – a devastating blow.

"Will I ever be picked to play for England again?" he fretted during his time spent out of the team. In the end he missed five months of cricket, returning during England's 2018 tour of New Zealand. The court case in August that year found Ben not guilty of the charges because he'd been defending other people who were being abused. The case, however, left its mark. It was not enough to be a champion on the pitch for England, Ben had to be careful about the situations he got into off the pitch as well.

⭐ CHAPTER 11 ⭐

It's Never Over

Time and time again, Ben had proven himself a match-winner for England. Yet six weeks after leading England to 2019 World Cup glory, even he was struggling to stop the Australians from claiming a decisive Ashes victory. The teams were playing at Headingley, with England already 2–0 down in the series. Defeat here and the Ashes would be lost.

England's first innings had been a disaster. They were bowled out for just 67 runs. Terrible! Ben had only made eight when he played a dreadful shot. He had foolishly chased a wide ball from James Pattinson, got the toe end of his bat on it and the ball flew to the slips where David Warner took it above his left shoulder.

OUT!

Ben had bowled a long spell when he was replaced by Jofra Archer, but four balls in, Jofra had to leave the field with cramp. "I'll do it," said Ben, finishing Jofra's over then continuing to bowl unchanged until the end of play.

The Headingley crowd, all 18,000 of them, were totally behind Ben.

"Stand up if you love Stokesy."

"Ben, Ben, Stokes! Stokes! Stokes!"

"Go on Eng-ur-land!"

Ben bowled 24.2 overs in total, taking three wickets for 56 runs. This left England needing 359 to win and keep the Ashes alive. Three hundred and fifty-nine was more than they'd ever chased before in Tests. A tall order, but Ben thought they could do it.

A tough challenge became even tougher

after both openers got out quickly. England were 15–2 and reeling. The two Joes – Denly and Root – settled England's nerves. And when Denly was out for 50, Ben strode in, aware that Australia's experienced spinner Nathan Lyon and their fast bowlers, Josh Hazlewood and Pat Cummins, were bowling really well.

To prove the point, a bouncer from Hazlewood hit Ben on the helmet with such force the stem guards were smashed off. Ben's left ear was ringing with the force of the blow but he wasn't going to show any sign of distress to his opponents, several of whom came over to check he was okay.

Out came England's team doctor Gurjit Bhogal to check if Ben had suffered concussion.

"Where are you?"

"Headingley, Leeds."

"Who are you?"

"Ben Stokes. Sheesh, Gurjit!"

Ben was getting agitated. He didn't want to

lose focus or show the Aussies any weakness. But Gurjit had to do his job, and the questions to test if Ben had suffered any memory loss continued.

"Come on, let's go. I'm absolutely fine. All good."

Gurjit did help tie the stem guards back on the helmet properly – Ben hadn't put them on correctly. This amused his batting partner Joe Root. "If they fall off and hit your stumps, you'll look a right idiot, Ben."

Ben finished the day on two not out and that evening got to see his wife Clare and their children. He refuelled with grilled chicken and one of his favourite treats – two raisin and biscuit chocolate bars. He'd expended a lot of energy and needed a whole lot more for the day ahead.

Into the next day and after 67 balls Ben had scored just three runs. He wasn't concerned. He had scored a century in the previous match, felt his feet were moving fine and he was seeing the ball well. The runs would come. But he was concerned when Joe charged down the pitch, the ball ballooned up off his bat then pad and David Warner dived to catch it. England still needed 200 more runs and their best batter was gone.

Warner and his fellow slip fielders kept making comments to try and get under Ben's skin.

"He'll give it away soon."

"Thinks himself a big tough guy."

"He's so lucky. He's not playing well."

But Ben was used to sledging and had got far better at not letting it affect his concentration.

He'd always liked batting with Jonny Bairstow and Jos Buttler. Jonny helped inject some pace to the England innings and he and Ben scored 86 runs together before Jonny lost his wicket. But Jos only faced nine balls before Ben ran him out.

Turning a ball away on the leg side, Ben had called Jos for a run without realising the Aussies had just placed Travis Head there as square leg fielder. Jos was a goner. Travis Head flicked the ball underarm swiftly onto the stumps. Out!

"What have I just done?" Ben thought as he took guard to the next delivery. He felt awful.

A few balls later, the crowd started applauding as Ben reached 50.

"He's not even raising his bat," laughed Marnus Labuschagne.

"Too right," thought Ben. "Nothing to celebrate yet." The Ashes were still on the line.

It looked like Ben's efforts would be for nothing after Chris Woakes, Jofra Archer and Stuart Broad all fell quickly. Out walked England's last batter, Jack Leach. England still needed 73 runs; it was a tall order and Australia were confident.

"C'mon boys, we got this."

"Stokes can't last."

"One more push and the Ashes are ours."

Ben eyed the field warily and walked up to Jack. "Just stay with me, Leachy," he muttered. "Five and one, or four and two." This meant Ben would try to face four or five balls each over, leaving Jack just one or two; Ben had to pick his shots extremely carefully to try to keep the strike as much as possible.

It was a glorious summer's day in Leeds. The temperature was pushing 30°C but Ben turned up the heat further with a series of outrageous strokes, including powerful pull shots and sweetly timed sixes straight down the ground. The pick of these was an incredible reverse sweep off Nathan Lyon when Ben was on 77. He switched his stance from left to right, swept the ball hard and it soared over the ropes. Incredible!

Headingley went wild as Ben's super-strike took England's target to within 50 runs of victory. The Australians were starting to feel the pressure now. In the sun-baked stands, the crowd were cheering every run scored. Hundreds of spectators were waving their shoes above their heads and chanting:

"Shoes off if you love England!"

"He's a freak!" exclaimed Jos Buttler back in the England dressing room.

Ben and Jack's target of 50 became 40, then 35. Whilst Ben was carving up the Australian attack, Jack stood firm each time he had to face deliveries from the express Australian pacemen. In between overs, he would meet Ben in the middle, sometimes punching gloves or polishing his glasses, which were in danger of steaming up every minute.

All around Britain, millions of people leaned closer to their radios or squinted hard at their screens. Could they really believe what they were seeing? Dare they hope?

THWACK!

Ben was on 96 when he hit a barnstorming drive which thundered into the boundary. As one, the crowd stood to cheer his hundred. Just like his half-century, Ben barely acknowledged it, just gave a little wave and nod. He still had work to do.

"A hundred for Ben Stokes. What a summer

he's having! What a cricketer he is!" roared Nasser Hussain on TV.

As Hazlewood bounded in to deliver the next ball, Ben dropped to one knee and swept the ball up, up and away. SIX! Ben smashed the following ball into the Western Terrace stand for another six. England now required just 21 to win.

Ben was exhausted but buoyed by the change in the Australian fielders. Their calls to each other were sharper, edgier than before, and they made a number of small errors.

"They're feeling the pressure," he thought, but so, too, was he. As the target dipped below 20, Ben simply couldn't watch when Jack faced a ball. He'd bow over his bat and look down at the ground. After all, one mistake and the game was over.

But it was Ben, not Jack, who gave the first chance when he sliced a shot that flew down towards third man. Aussie fielder Marcus Harris raced in, dived forward but failed to cling on to the ball. Ben's heart was in his mouth.

"Oh God . . . Wow, that was so close."

Eighteen, seventeen . . . the target dropped painfully slowly. The tension was almost unbearable. The 18,000-strong crowd went silent as a ball was bowled then became deafening when Jack Leach survived, or Ben scored runs. Two fours in a row off Pat Cummins took the runs needed down into single figures. Then, with England just two runs away from victory, Ben hit a sweep shot, didn't run, but when he looked up, saw Jack Leach sprinting towards him.

"Leachy! Nooo!"

Jack raced back but was well out of his ground as the ball was thrown to Nathan Lyon waiting by the stumps. It was a certain run out.

"Get back!" Ben's heart was pounding in his chest.

"Awww, heck!"

Nathan Lyon fumbled the ball and Jack was safe. The Australians had their heads in their

hands. So did many of the crowd in the stands –
the tension was off the scale.

Five balls later, Ben smoked the winning
runs through the covers, stood tall and roared.
Jack leapt into his arms. He may have only
scored a single out of their partnership of 74 but
England's number 11 had defended 16 other
deliveries heroically. Ben, though, had faced
219 deliveries and scored 135 runs including
eight big sixes and 11 fantastic fours.

The Australians were devastated but
congratulated Ben as his teammates raced
onto the ground.

"Take your time, take it all in, Ben," Joe Root
advised.

The crowd bounced and cheered wildly.
Some stood open-mouthed, amazed at the
spectacle.

"What have we just seen?"

"Only the greatest Test match innings, ever."

"Stokesy, you beauty!"

⭐ CHAPTER 12 ⭐

Taking a Break

In January 2020, Ben was playing Tests in South Africa where he became only the second England cricketer after Ian Botham to score 4,000 Test runs and take over 100 Test wickets. He should have been happy, but his family had just suffered a bitter blow. Ged, Ben's father, had been diagnosed with brain cancer.

Whenever Ben won a match or scored a century that year, he would raise his right hand and pull his middle finger back to mimic his dad's injury back in the 1980s. He did this to show his family he was always thinking of them. He withdrew from much of that summer's cricket to travel back to Christchurch. In December Ged died, leaving Ben, Deb and James, Ben's half-brother, devastated.

"Such a big inspiration to me had left the world and left me," Ben told the BBC.

He threw himself back into cricket but early 2021 proved tough. He played every game in England's draining 12-match tour of India in February and March, then joined the Rajasthan Royals in April for the IPL season. In the Royals' first match, versus the Punjab Kings, Ben dived to catch a shot from Chris Gayle but broke his left index finger. That was it for Ben and the 2021 IPL, and just like when he broke the index finger on his right hand in 2011, it needed more than one operation to repair.

The finger was painful but Ben was suffering even more mentally. He had been bottling up his frustrations, grief and emotions from events in his life for the past few years. The stresses of losing his father and being away from his young family so much were causing him problems. He was suffering from anxiety and terrible panic attacks.

"You just don't know whether you are going to be the same person when you wake up the next day," he said later in an interview.

Shortly before the summer Test series versus India, Ben made an important decision. "I will be taking an indefinite break from all cricket," he announced. No one, especially Ben, knew when he would return.

Cricket fans were stunned, but Ben needed to look after his mental health. He began talking about his feelings with Clare and other close friends. Then he sought out sessions with mental health professionals to learn and understand how he felt and what was wrong.

Ben didn't pick up a bat until October, after having a second operation on his finger that made it easier to move. When he did return in December, he talked openly about his mental health, how he still saw therapists from time to time, and encouraged other people to seek support if they were struggling. "Admitting you need help doesn't make you wrong or feeble," he argued, and in a 2022 Amazon Prime Sport interview, he explained how he continues to look after his mental health.

"Openly I speak to people, to doctors, take [anti-anxiety] medication – I'm not afraid to say that. Because I see it as a huge strength to be able to admit weakness."

People praised him for his honesty, including his old friend Joe Root. "It's quite powerful for people to see that sometimes it's okay not to be okay," Joe told the BBC. "It shows great leadership to put yourself out there and express some of the difficulties he's gone through."

★ CHAPTER 13 ★

Baz 'n' Ben

Joe Root had led from the front as England captain in more Tests (64) than any England skipper before him. But after tough series away to Australia and the West Indies, he'd had enough. He resigned as England captain in April 2022 after five years in what is a very demanding and draining job.

Joe's were big boots to fill and England turned to Ben alongside a brand new coach – Brendon 'Baz' McCullum. Ben was a huge fan of the former New Zealand captain and attacking batter who held the record for the most sixes hit in Test matches – a whopping 107.

Baz had never been a Test cricket coach and Ben had rarely captained. Some ex-players in the media thought the pair's lack of experience would end in disaster. They were wrong!

Ben and Baz messaged each other and then met. It turned out they were both thinking the same way. Both wanted to make it more fun for the players to play Test cricket and to stop games drifting away and becoming draws.

"Let's remove the fear of failure."

"Yeah. Losing sucks, but it's not the end of the world. I'd rather try to win and fail than not go for the win in the first place."

"Yup, and encourage the players to really enjoy themselves and be positive."

"Absolutely. Score quick runs and set attacking fields to grab wickets."

"Let's do it!"

To play this way meant taking big risks and increasing the chances of England losing some games, but Ben was excited by the challenge.

He loved Test cricket and figured that upping the excitement levels would be great for both players and fans.

Ben was determined to lead from the front. Before his first Test as captain, he appeared for Durham in a County Championship match. He thrashed an incredible 161 runs from 88 balls, including 17 sixes and 8 fours – that's 134 runs in boundaries. Ben had hit the most sixes in an innings since the official County Championship began in 1890! England's opponents had been alerted – this was how the new skipper wanted his team to play.

New Zealand were England's first opponents. They were world champions and included top players like Trent Boult and Kane Williamson. England won the first game with a great Joe Root century. But in the second, the Kiwis scored a whopping 553 in their first innings. There were mutterings from England fans in the crowd . . .

"We won't win playing with six slips instead of two."

"I knew Stokes would be a terrible captain."

"We'll be crying our eyes out at the end of this."

Fans' fears were unfounded, though. England won the game then romped to a 3–0 victory playing thrilling cricket, whether it was Jonny Bairstow's blistering hundred off just 77 balls or Jack Leach's 10 wickets in a match.
The players loved the bold new approach and how Ben and Baz kept things clear, simple and fun.

OUT went lots of boring meetings, dull practice sessions and worrying about your own scores or bowling figures.

IN came six-hitting competitions, encouraging each other, trying out new shots and skills, and having fun.

"Go on, Jimmy!"

"That's a six for James Anderson!"

"Ollie, you're next."

"Who's winning?"

"Stokesy's hit quite a few."

"He always does."

It wasn't all fun, fun, fun. Mindful of his own struggles, Ben also insisted that the England team had access to psychologists and other support. He was keen to create a happy, healthy workplace so that he and his teammates could perform at their best.

England continued on their rampage that summer, beating India and South Africa. In the Test against India, Jonny Bairstow scored amazing centuries (106 and 114) in both innings as England risked all to chase down 378 runs – the most they'd ever managed! After the winning runs were struck, a jubilant Jack Leach said, "Teams are perhaps better than us, but teams won't be braver than us."

Ben loved Leachy's words.

Before he was made captain, England had won just one of the previous 17 Test matches. After his first 11 matches in charge, England had won 10 – a stunning turnaround. A cricket journalist called Andrew Miller nicknamed their way of playing 'Bazball'. As much as Ben and Baz dislike it, that name has stuck!

In between the English summer and the winter tour to Pakistan was another ICC World Cup, this time in Australia. With Jos Buttler in charge of the T20 team, Ben had a break from captaincy. To be honest, he wasn't called into action much before the final, taking just six wickets and scoring 58 runs. This was mostly because Jos and Alex Hales at the top of the batting order were brilliant and blazed away. In the semi-final against India, for example, England didn't lose a wicket as they chased down 170 runs with four overs to spare.

In the final, though, versus a vibrant Pakistan bowling attack, England were under enormous pressure. Alex Hales was out for one run, Phil Salt for 10 and Jos for 26. Who did the team turn to?

Ben, of course!

No one knew how to time a run chase better,

especially under pressure. Ben and young Harry Brook, followed by Moeen Ali, kept the score ticking over, with Ben guiding the team home with an unbeaten 52 off 49 balls. It made England the first team to hold both the T20 and ODI World Cups at the same time.

Just two weeks later, Ben was back in charge, leading the England Test team to their first series in Pakistan since 2005–06. Pakistan had suffered some devastating floods and both teams hoped that an exciting series could provide some cheer.

Ben went further. He donated all his match fees from the series – worth about £45,000 – to the country's flood appeal to buy essential supplies. "The game has given me a lot in my life," he said. "I feel it's only right to give something back that goes far beyond cricket."

Pakistan were an exciting side themselves, blessed with batting maestros like Babar Azam and fast bowlers such as Shaheen Shah Afridi.

Pitches in Pakistan were traditionally flat and didn't help bowlers or fast-scoring batters. So, could Bazball thrive here?

The simple answer was YES!

In most Test matches, the first day is a real battle of nerves and wits as both teams struggle to get ahead. Between 250 and 320 runs is a typical total for the day as most Test sides score at 2.5–3.5 runs per over. In the first day of the first Test at Rawalpindi, Ben's side scored 506 runs at a rate of 6.75 per over. Phenomenal.

What made it even more amazing was that some of the team had been ill that morning and that only 75 overs could be bowled because of the short days in Pakistan in December. England's first innings total was 657 all-out. It included four century-makers, including young Harry Brook playing in only his second Test.

Ben 'only' made 41, although they came at an electrifying rate – in just 18 balls. But his most attacking act in the match was to end

England's second innings early. He set Pakistan a target of 343 in a day plus one session. Ben's bold declaration kept Pakistan in the game which also helped England get the wickets they needed to notch up an historic victory.

Commentating on TV, legendary Australian cricketer Mark Waugh said, "I don't think any other team in world cricket would have rolled the dice like that." Ben thought the win was "mind-blowing. The effort everyone's put in – I feel very honoured to lead these guys."

England won the second Test then completed a 3–0 clean sweep after their youngest ever player, Rehan Ahmed, took five wickets in an innings. Rehan had been selected for the third Test and was just 18 years old – what a start to his career!

During the run chase for the win, Ben tried but failed to hit his 108th six in Test cricket to pass his coach's world record. Despite failing, Ben was all smiles at recording such a remarkable series win. He was thrilled that his teammates had stepped up to play so well.

It wouldn't be until England toured New Zealand three months later that he got another chance to biff a six. It gave Ben an opportunity to catch up with relatives and childhood friends. He also got his certificate celebrating his call up to the Wellington youth cricket team when he was 12! Finally!

England won the first Test comfortably but lost the second by just one run in yet another gripping series. During the first match, Ben managed to loft the ball over the boundary to strike his 108th six and beat Baz's record, and with his coach looking on and applauding. To celebrate, Ben hit the next ball for six, too!

⭐ CHAPTER 14 ⭐

The Ashes 2023

June, 2023.

"Ashes?"

Moeen Ali looked at the single-word message from Ben Stokes that appeared on his smartphone. Moeen had known Ben for years and considered him a trusted friend, but he had retired from Test cricket two years earlier.

"Stokesy must be joking," he thought, so replied: *LOL*.

It was only after learning that England's first choice spinner, Jack Leach, was injured that he phoned Ben back. Moeen had loved watching the bold new way England were playing under Ben. "His mindset is so different to other captains. Everything is just so positive now. He's the kind of guy you want to play for."

The 2023 Ashes was one of the most eagerly anticipated series in world cricket. Australia were world champions, having defeated India in the World Test Championship final just five days before they faced England in the first Ashes Test at Edgbaston.

A mesmerising match see-sawed with both sides on top at different times. It looked like England would win late on the fifth day when Australia needed 54 runs and only had two wickets left. But Nathan Lyon and Australia's captain Pat Cummins batted them to victory. Cummins called the game, "The No. 1 Test I've ever played in".

Ben was "devastated but proud". England had shown they could compete with Australia. If they hadn't dropped so many catches or made

batting mistakes they could have
easily been one-up themselves.

The second Test proved tough for Ben and
England. Australia were on top with Mitchell Starc
and Pat Cummins bowling well. They set England
371 to win. England still needed 178 more runs,
with Ben and Jonny Bairstow batting when Jonny
left his crease thinking the over had finished and
was stumped in controversial fashion.

The crowd at Lord's are usually more
reserved and quieter than at other English
cricket grounds, but now there was uproar.
Boos rained down on the Australian team even
though what they had done was not against
the laws of the sport. Many fans, though,
thought it was not in the spirit of the game.

As Jonny stomped off, furious at what had
just happened, and Stuart Broad came to the
crease, Ben refocused. He had been in similar
positions before, such as at Headingley in 2019,
holding it all together whilst Australia pushed

for the win. With only four wickets left, Ben accelerated his run-scoring . . .

CRUNCH!

A big six off Cameron Green started changing the boos to cheers.

THWACK!

Another six by Ben, bigger than the first, came off the next ball.

SMASH!

Ben struck again, hooking another short delivery for his third six in a row.

Ben's big hitting had seen him race to a hundred despite his left knee giving him pain. Jonny, Joe and the rest of the team were out on the balcony applauding, too. It was another brilliant century from their inspirational captain.

Ben struck his fourth, fifth, sixth, seventh, eighth and ninth six of the innings – the most maximums scored in an Ashes innings by any England or Australian player. The target dropped to 90, then 80, then 70 . . .

Could the unthinkable be on? Could Ben repeat Headingley 2019?

Sadly, not this time. With the score on 301–6 and Ben on 155, he sliced a ball from Josh Hazlewood straight up into the air. Alex Carey snared the catch and the dream was over. Ben bowed his head and took an age to leave the crease.

"The end of a most magnificent innings," said Michael Atherton, commentating on TV.

The last England pair – Josh Tongue and Jimmy Anderson – got the target down to 43 runs before Josh was out. England were now 2–0 down in the series and hurting. Both teams had crucial injuries: Australia lost Nathan Lyon, and England Ollie Pope, both for the rest of the series.

Ben's troublesome left knee meant he couldn't bowl and reinforcements were needed for the third Test. England brought in Chris Woakes and Mark Wood. They both bowled brilliantly with

Wood taking 5–34 in the first innings. One of his deliveries was measured at 155.3 kilometres per hour – the fastest in Ashes history.

"It's great to see him smiling, running in and bowling rockets," said Ben of his good mate.

England's reply was faltering at 142–7 when Woody joined Ben at the crease and blazed a six, then a four, then another towering six . . . off the first three balls he faced!

Ben was suffering not only with his knee, but with a sore arm and a muscle strain in his bottom, but he, too, started hammering the Australian attack. England scored an incredible 95 in just 10 overs to get close to Australia's first innings score. Captain Fantastic top-scored for England again with 80 crucial runs – including five more sixes.

After Chris Woakes and Stuart Broad took three wickets each to keep Australia down to 227 all-out in their second innings, England were set 251 to win. The chase began confidently enough with Zak Crawley making 44, but then England started to falter. Ben couldn't repeat his heroics in the second innings, falling for just 13, and when Jonny Bairstow was out 12 balls later, England were reeling at 171–6.

Young Harry Brook scored a remarkably composed 75, then Chris Woakes and Mark Wood took on the challenge. Ben was so tense he couldn't watch. He drew cartoon pictures for a while then walked up and down the dressing room relentlessly. He far preferred being out in the middle as the action unfolded than this, looking on helplessly.

"Stop pacing, Ben. You're making me nervous."

"Can't help it – must have walked two kilometres by now!"

"See what it feels like now, Stokesy!"

England won, the series was alive, and next up was Manchester, where a roaring Old Trafford crowd were treated first to domination then disappointment.

Amazing Cricket Stars – Ben Stokes

On the second and third days of play, England went berserk with the bat. Zak Crawley scored an incredible 189, Jonny Bairstow a brutal 99, Joe Root 84, and there were half-centuries for Harry Brook, Moeen Ali and Ben. England amassed 592 – the highest total against Australia at home since 1985 – and at an incredible rate of 5.49 runs per over. Whilst Ben was batting, he spotted how Australia looked tired and were making small mistakes; they were rattled by England's all-action play.

England reduced Australia to 113 for four by the end of day three and fans felt it was just a matter of time before England levelled the series . . . but the weather and Australian batters had other ideas.

Marnus Labuschagne scored a brilliant 111 before rain fell to disrupt the fourth day and then completely wipe out the fifth. The game petered out into a draw and with that, Australia retained the Ashes. Ben was gutted but still upbeat at the great cricket his side had played.

England named an unchanged team for the fifth and final Test at the Oval in London. For the first time in the series, Ben lost the toss and on an overcast day Pat Cummins asked England to bat.

It didn't go well.

England were in trouble and it took their young gun Harry Brook's 85 to bail them out. Then, poor Moeen Ali tore his groin muscle so couldn't bowl. The rest of the attack worked really hard as the game see-sawed back and forth, just like the whole series.

Ben came in to bat at number three in England's second innings as Mo was still suffering. The skipper, Zak Crawley and Joe Root all helped power England to a commanding total. Australia would need 384 to win and mid-Test, Stuart Broad announced this would be his 167th and last Test match – he was retiring from all cricket. Ben knew before the rest of the cricketing world because Stuart had spoken to him beforehand.

After lunch on the very last day of the series, it looked like Stuart's farewell would be ruined. Australia had passed 250 comfortably – just 130 or so runs to go. They still had seven wickets remaining and plenty of overs to score the winning runs. Ben and the rest of the England team summoned up one last crucial burst of energy.

Chris Woakes bowled beautifully and so, despite his groin injury, did Moeen Ali. In just 19 balls, the pair took four wickets as Australia's middle order were ripped out. Ben had been practising his bowling that morning, prepared to risk further injury if his team needed him, but they didn't! When Moeen took Pat Cummins' wicket, Australia were 294–8 and Ben decided it was time to bring Broady on for his final ever spell. He didn't disappoint.

First Todd Murphy, then Alex Carey fell to catches by Jonny Bairstow off balls bowled by Stuart Broad. England had won by 49 runs and drawn the series!

After going 2–0 down to the world champions, Ben's boys had roared back to be the better side in the final three games. Ben was rightly proud of all his players and the exciting comeback they'd staged. He paid tribute to his two retiring players, Stuart Broad and Moeen Ali (who was retiring for a second time after answering Ben's call for help for the Ashes).

Moeen said, "I'm done. If Stokesy messages me again, I'm going to delete it!"

Unlike Moeen, Ben was definitely carrying on, planning surgery on his knee so that he could star in many more games to come. For all his personal achievements and match-winning moments, he may become best remembered for transforming the England Test team into an exciting, memorable side.

After the fourth Test, Ben had spoken to his team in the dressing room. His words were stirring.

"The reward for your work isn't what you get, it's what you become. And what we've managed to become is a team that people will remember. Regardless of how the series ends up, people will always talk about us."

And plenty of people will be talking about Ben Stokes . . . for a long, long time.

Ben Stokes Fact File

(as of January 2024)

Born: 04/06/1991, Christchurch, New Zealand

Tests
97 matches

6,117 runs, 197 wickets, 102 catches

13 hundreds, 30 fifties

716 fours, 124 sixes

ODIs
114 matches

3,463 runs, 74 wickets, 55 catches

5 hundreds, 24 fifties

282 fours, 109 sixes

T20 Internationals
43 matches

585 runs, 26 wickets, 22 catches

0 hundreds, 1 fifty

42 fours, 22 sixes

**Turn the page for a sample of
Amazing Cricket Stars – Virat Kohli!**

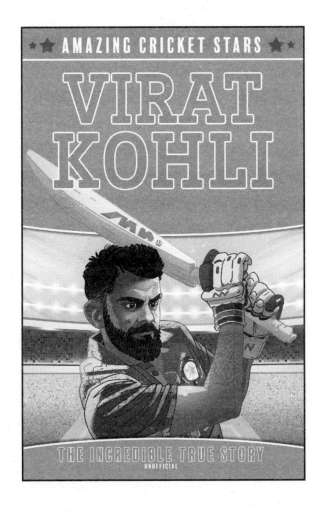

⭐ CHAPTER 1 ⭐

Quickfire Kohli

18 May 2016

A packed crowd at the M. Chinnaswamy Stadium in the Indian city of Bengaluru were hushed as Sandeep Sharma sprinted in to bowl. Facing was the Royal Challengers Bangalore's captain and star batter, Virat Kohli. It was the first ball of his innings and it was a must-win game for his team.

THWACK!

The ball rocketed off Virat's bat and sped away over the damp grass. A Kings XI Punjab fielder lunged for it, but it had raced past before he'd even completed his dive.

Four!

The home crowd exploded with cheers. Some fans glanced down at their phones to read the text commentary:

Kohli needs no sighters. Stands tall and punches that between cover and point. Shot of a man in the form of his life. Beautiful.

Virat was indeed in great form. He was having a brilliant season in the world's biggest Twenty20 (T20) competition, the Indian Premier League. With just 20 overs for each team, batters scoring hundreds are rare. In fact, in the 2014 IPL, there had been just three centuries in all the 60 games played. Virat in 2016 had already scored three himself, the last coming just four days earlier when he and South African maestro AB de Villiers had scored an incredible 229 between them . . . in just 107 balls. A-maz-ing!

Their RCB teammate, West Indian hard-hitter Chris Gayle, labelled the pair Batman and

Superman, and he should know – Chris held many records for rapid scoring in T20 and ODI cricket and he set off fast at the top of the innings . . . with Virat alongside him.

Torrential rain had shortened the match to just 15 overs (90 balls) per side – not long to build any sort of score. Virat was mindful of this. At least there was a game on, he thought. Rain had washed out a crucial match that stopped RCB from making it to the 2015 IPL (Indian Premier League) final.

Virat had learned how even in a short match, there were times to defend as well as attack. He was famous for his effortless flicks and other leg side shots, but his favourite stroke was the cover drive. "There is no better feeling, especially against the quick bowlers, when you drive them with the full stride, on the rise, with a high elbow," he said in a 2015 interview. And that's what he did in the sixth over, followed by a cheeky reverse sweep for another four the next ball.

"Yes, Virat, YES!" boomed Chris Gayle. The big West Indian liked what he saw.

Virat, though, was wincing in pain. He had suffered an injury whilst fielding in the previous match. Beneath his batting glove just past the '269' tattoo on the back of his left hand (Virat was the 269th Test cricketer to play for India) were eight stitches in the webbing between his thumb and forefinger. The stitches throbbed every time his bat connected with the ball.

But Virat blanked out the pain. Few players could match his intense focus or hunger for runs. He crunched another four and then, in the seventh over, hit a seven! The delivery from KC Cariappa was a no-ball meaning one was added to RCB's total and the ball re-bowled. But the batting side also gain any extra runs the batter strikes and Virat swung hard, launching the ball into the crowd . . . SIX!

Cariappa's next ball was blazed down the ground by Virat for another maximum.

The crowd were off their feet.

"Six! Six! From King Kohli!"

"Go RCB. Smash them!"

"Kohli, Kohli, Kohli, Kohli!"

Shortly afterwards, Virat raised his bat. He'd reached 50 in just 28 balls. "Surely, I can't get a 100 in 15 overs?" he thought to himself . . . although it would be fun trying.

Virat had joined Royal Challengers Bangalore as a young cricketer in 2008 for the cut-price fee of $30,000 (over £23,600). At an IPL auction today, he would go for millions. Despite offers to join other IPL teams, he had stayed with RCB ever since and had actually played in the very first IPL match, against the Kolkata Knight Riders. There, he'd watched on open-mouthed as Brendon 'Baz' McCullum launched an astonishing assault on his team's bowlers. The New Zealand big hitter pummelled 158 runs in a 20-over game.

Virat loved Baz's aggression, but went on to develop his own T20 game, which included becoming one of the most effective runners between the wickets; he could often turn a likely single into two runs. And Virat mostly played 'proper' cricket shots, using all his experience from Test cricket. So, no scoops and few slogs . . . well, not until the very end of the innings.

That said, he could still play spectacularly. He blasted three massive sixes – over long-on, long-off and midwicket – in the 10th over to reach 69, and then added 24 in the next seven balls as he carved shots all round the ground. He could barely feel the pain in his hand now, and the noise in the crowd grew and grew . . .

"Virat's into the nineties, now."

"Kohhhhhhhhliiiiii!"

"He's done it again! SIX!"

"Oh my, that's landed high in the second tier of the stand. That's HUGE!"

Another boundary in the 14th over, this time a four, saw Virat leap with joy. Yes! He had struck his fourth IPL century that season.

He turned towards the RCB team dugout and pumped his fist wildly.

He continued his celebrations by striking the next ball for six (the eighth of his innings) followed by a four which took him to 4,002 IPL runs, the first player to cross the 4,000-mark. When he was out, for 113, the whole ground stood to applaud. Virat's rapid innings had taken just 50 balls and included 48 runs in sixes and 48 runs in fours. WOW!

RCB posted a formidable score of 211 – that's over 14 runs per over. Faced by such an onslaught, the Kings XI Punjabi collapsed. Their whole team only managed to score seven runs more than Virat did by himself!

RCB reached the IPL final but finished runners-up. Virat, however, won the IPL's coveted Orange Cap for the competition's leading run-scorer. He'd driven, pulled, glanced and smashed a total of 973 runs: 125 more than Australian legend David Warner in second place, and with his pal AB de Villiers 286 runs behind, in third.

But those 973 runs were only part of Virat's 2016 story. He also became the first batter to score over 600 runs in Twenty20 internationals (T20i), and smashed 739 runs – including three centuries – in one day internationals (ODIs) for India. As captain of India's Test team throughout 2016, he amassed 1,215 Test runs, including four centuries.

Add all these feats together and you have a truly astonishing total of 3,568 runs in major competitions in 2016. What a year! What a player!

How did Virat Kohli become such a titan of T20s, Tests and ODIs? How was he able to drive himself on, year after year, to stay at the top of cricket in all three formats of the game?

It all started in India's biggest city . . .

★ CHAPTER 2 ★

A Son of Delhi

More than 30 million people live in and around
Delhi and on 5 November 1988, Virat Kohli
became one of them. This giant metropolis is
split into 11 separate districts or territories.
One is New Delhi, which is the capital of the
country and its neighbouring territory, West Delhi.

Split by the Sahibi river, West Delhi is home
to two million people. If you take a short walk
north from the river, through the bustling streets
teeming with people, cars and motorbikes,
you'll find a locality called Paschim Vihar.
There, close to the busy Rohtak Road
expressway, are the Punjabi Bagh Apartments

where the Kohlis lived. This Punjabi Hindu family numbered five: Saroj (mum) and Prem (dad), their daughter, Bhawna, and two sons, Vikas and Virat.

Virat's father, Prem, hadn't always lived in Delhi. He had been born 850 kilometres south in the state of Madhya Pradesh, in a city officially called Murwara, but which is better known as Katni because of its location on the banks of the Katni river. Prem's brother still lives in the old family home, and Prem's sister, Asha Kohli, was elected mayor of Katni. Searching for more opportunities and a better life, Prem made his way to Delhi and became a lawyer and businessman.

A keen cricket fan, Prem was delighted when both his sons started playing – not that his youngest boy needed much encouragement. Virat was only three when he first held a toy bat and asked his father to bowl a soft ball at him again . . . and again . . . and again.

"Another ball. Another!"

"Now, now, Virat. That's enough. I'm tired."

"Vikas, you bowl at your brother. Gently, though."

"Okay, Father."

"Then both of you must wash before dinner."

"Yes, Mother."

Cricket wasn't the only sport Virat fell in love with. By the time he went to the Vishal Bharti Public School, he also enjoyed football. However, like many of his classmates, he mostly played cricket in the playground or in any open spaces they could find after school.

Street or gully cricket might use a wooden packing crate or a stack of bricks as stumps. And instead of an actual hard cricket ball, a tennis ball with wicked bounce would be bowled. Sometimes, a tennis ball would be wound round with insulation or duct tape to make a tapeball, which mimicked a real seaming and swinging cricket ball.

Even at a young age, Virat thirsted for

a challenge. Not content with playing gully cricket with kids of his own age, he often joined Vikas' gang of friends. Vikas was seven years older than Virat but was a good older brother to him . . . well, most of the time. Vikas' friends put up with Vikas' mop-haired younger brother, especially as Virat was a bundle of energy who would happily field wherever he was told to. He just wanted to be involved in the game.

Virat's sharp reactions and timing proved exceptional from a very early age. Like many young gully cricketers, Virat gripped the bat with a very strong bottom hand. This helped him get on top of the ball, which would often rear up sharply after it hit the rock-hard concrete or sun-baked ground they were playing on. Vikas' mates struggled to get him out.

"Your brother is so good at batting, Vikas."

"I know, I know."

"No, he's *too* good for us. It's embarrassing not being able to get a little kid out."

A Son of Delhi

The older boys started leaving the game just as it was Virat's turn to bat. Not fair!

Virat, Vikas and millions of other cricket-mad Indians in the 1990s and early 2000s idolised Sachin Tendulkar. A genius batter, Sachin scored century after century for India in both one day internationals and Test matches. He was unstoppable. Virat followed his every move excitedly on TV and in the news.

"Vikas! Vikas! Wake up! Tendu has scored another century."

"What, Virat? I was . . ."

"*Against* Sri Lanka. 148. That's his fourteenth Test hundred."

"Oh, go away, little brother."

"And his third against Sri Lanka this year."

When sixteen-year-old Sachin started out playing international cricket, he was placed under the wing of an older player, a fast bowler called Atul Wassan. The pair played in the Indian side that won the 1990–91 Asia Cup – a one day international competition. Atul and Sachin even lived together for a time in England, but only on Atul's strict instructions: "I cook, you clean!"

Atul played just four Test matches and nine ODIs for India before injuries stopped him progressing further. He did, though, play cricket for Delhi for 13 years until, in 1998, he decided to retire. One of his Delhi teammates, Rajkumar Sharma, who batted and bowled off-spin, was an aspiring coach. Together, the pair decided to open a new cricket school in West Delhi for children who dreamt of being the 'next Sachin Tendulkar'.

"Father, look at this news."

"Calm down, Virat."

"But, Father, look, it's amazing. *Look*."

"Okay, okay. What is it?"

"The West Delhi Cricket Academy is opening for boys wanting to play cricket better."

"Interesting . . ."

"In Vikaspuri. That's so close to us."

"No, it's more like five or six kilometres away, Virat."

"Can we go, Father? Please?"

"We'll see, Virat. Better tell Vikas, as well."

On 30 May 1998, Prem Kohli and his two sons travelled the five or so kilometres south to the Saviour Convent School cricket ground in Vikaspuri. It was the opening enrolment day of Atul and Rajkumar's West Delhi Cricket Academy (WDCA). A heatwave had engulfed the whole of India and temperatures were well above a sweltering 40°C. The Kohli boys were just two of 250 young hopefuls, all wishing to receive coaching at the new academy. At the end of the day, Virat was enrolled in the cricket school.

END OF SAMPLE

About the Author

CLIVE GIFFORD is an award-winning author of more than 200 books, including the official guide to the ICC Cricket World Cup 2019. His books have won the Blue Peter Children's Book Award, the Royal Society Young People's Book Prize, the School Library Association's Information Book Award and Smithsonian Museum's Notable Books For Children. Clive lives in Manchester within a short walk of Lancashire's Old Trafford cricket ground.

Read more sports books from Red Shed!

Amazing Cricket Stars

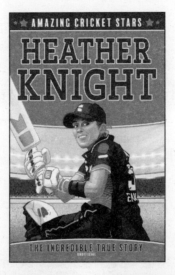

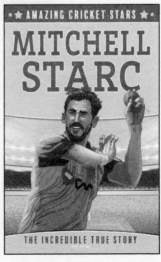

Incredible Sports Stories

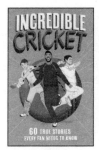   

Amazing Football Facts